W9-DDE-452

this book is dedicated
to Ellie Nichol

the ghost horse of the mounties

by sean o huigin

ILLUSTRATIONS BY BARRY MOSER

DAVID R. GODINE · PUBLISHER · BOSTON

First U. S. edition published in 1991 by
DAVID R. GODINE, PUBLISHER, INC.
Horticultural Hall, 300 Massachusetts Avenue
Boston, Massachusetts 02115

Library of Congress Cataloging in Publication Data
o huigin, sean, 1942–
The ghost horse of the mounties.
Summary: In this narrative poem, a storm overwhelms
the Royal Canadian Mounties, scattering their horses
in all directions and resulting in the mysterious
disappearance of one horse.
1. Royal Canadian Mounted Police—History—Juvenile
poetry. 2. Children's poetry, Canadian. [1. Royal
Canadian Mounted Police—Poetry. 2. Horses—Poetry.
3. Canadian poetry. 4. Narrative poetry] I. Moser,
Barry, ill. II. Title.
PR 9199.3.037G46 1991 811'.54 87-46287
ISBN 0-87923-721-X

First edition
Printed in the United States of America

the ghost horse of the mounties

imagine if you will the empty plains
imagine if you will a sultry summer night
imagine if you will a brilliant edge
of gold on the horizon
and a silence getting deeper all the time

listen now
the time is long ago
listen close and let yourself go back
imagine if you can that you're a young man
standing in the prairie grass
alone

it's summer's june
a june of heat and silence now
it's summer's june
in 1874

the northwest territories then
it's manitoba canada right now
a little place called dufferin
those days
and gathered there a group of men
who someday would be famous
round the world

listen now
there is no wind to hear
look again and see horizon's gold
a golden line made by the setting sun
a line that moves and changes as you
10 watch

look up and see the evening sky
dark blue
a clearness in the air you almost
feel
behind you
to the east horizon's dark
an almost black that changes as
you turn
to that dark blue above then lighter
down to that fine line of fiery gold

imagine if you can
you're a young man
standing in the prairie grass
alone
a little distance over a small rise
a group of wagons
tents and men
are formed

and most of all
a little way beyond
two hundred fifty horses
lift their heads

their ears prick up
they wave them back and forth
their nostrils flare as each one
smells the air

now try
try hard
imagine now with all the
might you have
imagine that a certain horse
is you

a slim black horse
with muscles strong and
hard
a white maned horse
long silky tail to match

you're standing in the long
tall prairie grass
you've travelled many miles
from the east
you rode on trains
you carried men
you pulled the wagons
and tonight you rest

tonight
you rest
but why then is a
restlessness amongst you and
your friends
why does the empty sky
give no delight

together now you sniff
the air again
what is it that you seem
to smell that scares
together now you listen
to no sounds
you twitch your tail
you shake your mane
and all the other horses
stamp their feet

imagine now
and find a special name
a horse's name that will
be yours alone
a magic name that's faster
than a shooting star
and brighter than the
full white moon at night

imagine now
imagine that young man
who's standing in the prairie grass
alone
for he's the man who rides you in
the day
and he's the man who combs your
mane at night

and listen now
what is it that you hear
a whispering of words from
over there
the sound the young man's thinking
in your head
that special wind that blows
from you to him
and back
and carries in between
the thoughts you think
and no one else
can hear

you feel together
something strange
a much too stillness
settling on the night
you feel the cold
the shivers running
up and down the
other's spine
you feel the fear
that comes
for while the night
is still and hot
it creeps inside
your souls and
leaves a chill

imagine now
the young man looking
up
to see a lonely prairie
hawk that soars
and in the east
the evening star comes out

he turns
the young man turns
and looks from east
to west
and where the gold line
was are mounting clouds
marching black and mountains
in the air with two
no
three bright golden rays
which shoot out from
behind then
disappear

and from the west
a breeze begins to stir
the prairie grass
begins a silent dance
the breeze becomes a
wind
the grasses sing with
hushing sounds
and in the air
the moving faster
racing air a water
smell and thunder
sounds are borne

imagine now
the horses shake
their heads
your white mane
tosses
streaking in the
wind

you hear a sound
a flapping sound
a sound like giant
eagle wings
you rise up on your
hind legs
wave your front
and whinny to
fight off what
it might
be

the young man whirls
a sound that's more
than thunder comes
to him
it seems as though the
racing clouds
the water mountains
rolling through
the prairie skies
have grown wings
and he can hear
the beating
as they race his
way

but something's strange
the flapping of this
sound comes strongest when
in brief moments
the wind will stop
as though it had to
take a breath
to gain some strength
before it blew
again

he runs
he races for the rise
that hides the camp
and looking down
he sees the other
men
running through
the flapping tents
the tents that seem
to open wings
and try to fly
away

you lift your head
and standing on
the ridge above
you see the young
man blown by the
wind
his long hair
streaking out
just like your
mane

you see him look
and turn to stare
the way he does
and there upon
the ground are
giant birds
like monstrous
vultures flapping
at the other
men
you neigh and call
the herd about
they whirl and
stomp
then whinny at
you
laughing horses'
laughs
and then you see
the birds are
tents
uprooted by the
wind
and all the men
now try
to tie them down

imagine now
that you are with
those men
you run between
the flapping
and their shouts

they're special men
the very first
the very new
beginnings of
the northwest
mounted police

and here they are
their scarlet jackets
dodging through
the growing dark
their pointed long
moustaches
blowing in the
wind
their leader
Colonel French
from whom they
copied their
moustache
shouting out
the orders to
restore the
camp

and here they are
bringing law and
order to the west
sent to stop
the whiskey runners
from the united
states

and here they are
fighting their
first battle
with the
wind

the young man runs
he joins the other
mounties in
the camp

one by one the
giant birdlike
tents are tamed
tied down and
heaving as if
out of breath

then he hears you
he hears your
frightened whinny
and looks up

the other horses
laughing they may
be
but still they're
nervous
something's still
amiss

he comes to you
the young man comes
and strokes your
neck
he pats your side
and whispers in
your ear

you calm
your sides are
heaving
heaving like the
tents but now
you're getting
steadier

his hand is soft
his gentle thoughts
are soothing in
your mind

imagine now
it's almost
ten o'clock
the huge black
clouds have covered
up the sky
you look around
the dark is
everywhere
and then

and then the
wind is gone

you stand there
with the young man
with the horses
and the camp
is still

and then

and then you feel
upon your flank
a huge wet drop

the rain has come
and drop by drop
it's falling from
the sky
and thicker comes
and faster
till you cannot
see the horse
beside you
cannot see the
tents or men

the young man goes
he races for the camp
he cannot see
and fumbles for
his tent

listen now
and hear the
pouring rain
listen as the
water forms in
rivulets and
gurgles round
your feet

your tail is
wet and heavy
and your mane
hangs down in
strands

listen now
listen to the
somehow silence
that is in
the air

there's still
no wind

and now
and now from
out the night
from out the
clouds a fireball
descends
a brilliant and
enormous light
that shows up
every raindrop
like a photograph
and then
the thunder
comes

the roar that
crashes and rips
up the night

listen now
the sound so
loud you cannot
even hear

the rumbling sound
as though the
earth was grinding
up
the cracking sound
of every tree in
all the world
splitting all at
once
the deep black
roar as all the
clouds mount up
like giants
rising from
the deep
and hissing as
they drop on you
in waterfalls
so strong you
cannot stand

you're in the
mud
the wind is back
and screaming
through the night

the other horses
mill and neigh
they slip like
you and struggle
to their feet

imagine now
imagine how the wind
builds up
and builds a solid
wall of rain
that hems you
in

imagine if you can
a night of light
a black night full
of roar and rain
when lightning
never stops
from ten o'clock
that summer's night
till six o'clock
the morning next
all the lightning
ever thought of
anywhere
illuminates the
land

above you see the
tops of clouds
flashing dully
with a steely grey
you know that in
between them
sharp thin bolts
of light are
flashing and
reflected on their
hills

imagine now
all around the
country's edge
a jagged line of
dancing bolts
clouds of steam
burst where
they touch the
ground
then across
sky itself a horde
of giant lightning
cracks that
make it seem
the universe
has split

imagine if you can
inside a tent
the young man huddles
scrunches up to his
companions
six men squeezed together
close as they can be

outside it seems
some monstrous beast
is pawing at the
canvas walls
its growls and
roars are pawing
at their hearts

through the canvas
water pours
each gust of wind
will slap it
through like
squeezing out a
sponge

and all the time
the light outside
grows dimmer
brighter
brilliant flashes
seem as if they'll
rip the tents

and over all
the howling
hissing
moaning
screaming
wind

imagine now
the horses bunched together
manes and tails are
blowing in the wind
a circle's formed
their heads are down
if looked at from
above their blowing
hair would make them
seem some huge and
furry insect
writhing in the mud

imagine now
you're huddled up
your wet skin feels
the shivers of your friends

and on it goes
two hours now the world
has turned to roar and
mud
when suddenly
for a small moment
silence falls
illuminated still by
sheets of light

and then

and then across the plain
like giant legs and
crashing beast
huge bolts of lightning
marching towards
the camp

imagine now
the horses raise their heads
imagine if you can a shudder
running through the herd
at once

your ears in fear laid back
upon your head
your nostrils wide
your eyes as open as your
eyes can be
your neighbours' too
and in their eyes you see
reflected cracks of
light taking on a redness
from their veins

then all at once a wild
scream goes up
no wind this time but
terrors from the herd

as if it were one body
altogether all the horses
rise
their front hoofs pounding at
air from where the lightning
comes

and on that summer's midnight
marked by thundrous crashes
and light bursts
the horses flee
they rip their tethers from
the ground
they smash into the corral
walls and pound them to
the earth

imagine now
the young man in his tent
the quick surprise as
that small time of quiet
comes
and then the mighty roar
of twelve gigantic
footsteps marching
cross the plain

imagine now
a scream that tears the
night
a scream that sounds unearthly
as though all the hidden
demons of the land were
loose at last

and then

and then another thunder
shaking all the ground
a thunder not from out
the sky but pounding on
the earth

imagine now
imagine that young man
whose head snaps up
whose eyes now open wide
as in his mind he sees
the horses now
the wild frightened horses
are stampeding

imagine if you can
that midnight night
the mounties racing from
their tents to try to
calm the horses

but too late

the herd is loose
imagine as they race with
fear that blinds them
race across a land they
do not see

imagine now the men who leap
for some of them
the men who try to slow
them down
but tossed aside and
trampled underneath

imagine if you will
the young man
running towards the herd
imagine that he calls
your name
imagine that he looks about
searching
calling
trying to reach you before
the horses knock you
down and crush
you in the mud

imagine now
imagine as you flee from
everything
that somewhere
suddenly beneath your fear
you hear the young man shout
you feel his pain
and in your mind for one small
moment you see him
as knocked to earth and
kicked about his head

but then he's gone
and all that's left
is fear

imagine now
the pounding of your hoofs
imagine now the mud that
flies behind
imagine now
the roaring and the grumbling
beast that seems
so close to catching you

your legs reach out
your heart is pounding
harder than it ever has
before
your eyes are open white
and froth flies from your
mouth as every leap you
make must be much larger
than the last

you stumble over gopher
holes
your left front knee is
skinned against a rock
and still you race
because you know behind
you is some evil
thing that surely will
destroy you if you stop

and then just as you crest
a rise
a brilliant flash of lightning
lights the land around
and there out in the distance
there in front of you on
that huge treeless plain
you see a giant silver
snake that waits for you

48

imagine now
beside your head
a flash of golden
lightning and a
smell of smoke
one pounding crash
of thunder
and your mind goes
blank

listen now
and hear the buzzing bees
listen now
and hear the song the sparrow
sings
feel a warm breeze gentle on
your body's side
then lift your head
and get up on your feet

the storm has gone
its rumbles faintly can be
heard rolling over east's
horizon
there again the dark clouds show
their gold rimmed edge
and wait the rising sun

listen now
and hear the summer's
morning sounds
look now to the east and see
the bright sun rise
stand on top your little hill
and turn where last night visions
of a serpent grew and see now
a great river in its blue

pembina water
that's the name the river is
curling through the prairie
as you see
pembina river
water river
prairie river full now from
the rain

your mane is dark
your tail is caked with mud
the prairie dogs stand up and
whistle
shake their tails at you

a bit away two antelopes
look up
their brown white colours
flashing in the light
above a hawk who circles on
the morning air
surveying all the markings
from the night

imagine if you will
you're moving down
moving towards the
river in the early
light
your leg is sore
your body's streaked
with drying mud
your head hangs down
exhausted as you
limp your way

you reach the river's
edge and find a shallow
pool
the water gently circles
in a soothing swirl

you have a drink
then lie down in the
water rolling
cleaning off the mud
and feeling good

the gentle curl of water
washes off the dirt
the coolness of the water
wakes you up

you feel refreshed
you heave onto your feet
and shake yourself
the water flies
creates a little rainbow in
the early sun

imagine if you can
the morning camp
the tents now still
and drying in the
breeze
the ground all trampled
from the horses' race
the men stand weary
ready to begin their
search

the last gold line on
clouds' horizon bursts
in brightness as the
sun comes up

and from the tents
the moans of six men
injured
trampled in the night

and the young man
the man who combed your
horse's mane
the young man lies his
head in bandages
the worst of all

the young man lies
so still it seems he
might be dead
and still within his
tortured dreams he
calls your name and tries
to stop you fleeing
through the night

long days the men
go out
searching for the tracks
the horses left
ten miles
twenty
thirty five they go
and one by one the
animals are found

slowly they're brought
back to camp
each man finds his own
and cleans it up

two hundred fifty
horses fled that
night
and all are gathered
back this time
but one

imagine now
the horse that's you
imagine how as days
go by you wander searching
trying to find the young man
the camp
the other horses
calling with the wind and
stamping ground in your
frustration

imagine now
as weeks go by
the times you think you
see a scarlet flash and
go
gallop over prairie rolls
and plains
but no
each time you reach the
place you thought
there's only emptiness

imagine now
the loneliness you feel
imagine as the prairie dogs
look up at you
your head hangs lower
and your hoofs are split

imagine now
a group of buffalo
their great black bodies
shadows on the plain
imagine how they snort
and shake their heads
as though discussing
all your sadness
just between themselves

imagine now
imagine as the years go by
you wander miles round and
round the plain

your hair is whitening on
your body
your tail and mane are
growing thin

imagine now
you wander one day slowly
over a small rise
and something in your
vision makes you lift
your head
some old old smell that
wafts into your nose
some old old echo of
a rumbling and a flashing
light
they make you stop

they call to you and
lead you down the hill
they call to you and lead
you to a certain spot
a certain little mound
upon the plain

and there you stop
an old and broken
wooden cross is leaning
on the ground
and somewhere deep inside
your head you hear a voice
a young man's voice that
calls to you
that welcomes you
that weeps with joy to
find that you've
come back

imagine now
the weariness you feel
imagine now
you sink upon your knees
imagine now
you rest upon your side
you stretch your neck
and gently close your
eyes

imagine now
imagine a soft summer
breeze that blows
imagine that you open
just a little your one
eye
and see on the horizon
a bright line of gold
a moving line
a line that comes toward
you and draws behind a
curtain of dark clouds

imagine now
imagine that a burst of
gold comes forward from
the line
imagine that a burst of
gold will touch the mound
beside you and you see
standing in the golden light
a young man scarlet jacketed
with pants steel grey
a glistening helmet
on his head
and brown boots on
his feet

imagine now
the young man rises
towards the clouds
his hand outstretched
his smile calling you

imagine now
you sigh and close your
eye
but just before the last
of sight has left
you see a shaft of
cloud that breaks through
the gold line and stretches
races
stretches
bunches up then grows a
head
a horse's head and legs
and flowing mane
a white mane long
and matched by
silky tail

imagine now
your spirit rises to
that horse the young
man mounts
behind the line of fiery
gold a burst of light
a rumble like some
marching drums
and then across the
prairie sky you soar
his helmet glistening
your eyes alight
and all these hundred
years and more
whenever young folks join
the mounties march
your spirit rises on its
cloud legs
paws the air
the ghost horse of the
mounties and the young
man's soul
salute

afterword

this story is
a fantasy
but based on
fact

when the northwest
mounted police were
first formed
and first camped
at dufferin
manitoba
in june of 1874
there was a storm
in which the lightning
is reported to have
not stopped from 10 pm
to 6 am

two hundred fifty
horses did stampede
and all were found
but one

six men were injured
one seriously about
the head

the uniform described
is the original
dress uniform
the white helmets also
had a showy brass
spike on top